Listen Up!

by Paul Beck

Welcome to the Lab!
To start building your
Voice Changer right away,
turn to page 18!

Listen Up!

If you have questions or comments about this product, send e-mail to info@smartlabtoys.com or visit www.smartlabtoys.com.

Edited by Ben Grossblatt
Written by Paul Beck
Art direction and packaging design by Scott Westgard
Book interior art direction and illustrations by Eddee Helms
Designed by Amy Redmond
Assembly illustrations by John Laidlaw
Product photography by Keith Megay
SmartLab® character photography by Craig Harrold
Product development by Chris Tanner and Lillis Taylor
Production management by Katie Stephens
Project management by Beth Lenz
Facts checked by Melody Moss
Image research by Melody Moss
Additional research by Eve Florin and Fran Tooke

Image credits: Page 6: Vocal folds, courtesy of the Center for Voice at Northwestern University; Larynx model © 3B Scientific GmbH, Hamburg, Germany, www.3Bscientific.com, used with permission. Page 11: Von Kempelen's voice machine courtesy of Prof. Hartmut Traunmüller, Institute for Linguistics, Stockholm University; Microphone © Stanley Coutant, courtesy of Prof. Stanley Coutant, Pasadena City College. Page 15: Speakers on pole (background), courtesy of Southern California Sound Image Inc.; Speaker disassembled © Levi Lansing, courtesy of Levi Lansing.

Every effort has been made to correctly attribute all the material reproduced in this book. We will be happy to correct any errors in future editions.

Printed, manufactured, and assembled in China.

Listen Up! is part of the SmartLab® *You Build It Voice Changer* kit. Not to be sold separately.

10 9 8 7 6 5
0-9748486-4-6
05258

VOICE CHANGER

Your Voice Changer changes more than just your voice. It also changes sound into electrical signals, then it changes the electrical signals into computer code, and then it does the whole thing in reverse.

It all starts with the sound of your voice!

Sound is waves that are created by vibration. Everything that vibrates makes sound.

When something vibrates — like a metal bell, or the string on a guitar — it pushes against the air molecules around it. Those molecules push against the molecules around *them*, which push against the molecules around them. After each push, the molecules bounce back to where they were. Each vibration makes a pulse, a pushing-together and pulling-apart of air molecules. The pulses travel outward in waves.

SOUND

Sound waves spread out like the ripples a pebble makes when it lands in a puddle.

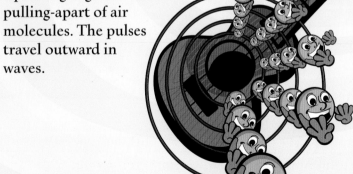

3

Your body has special sound wave detectors! They're in your ears. When sound waves reach your ears, the pulses push against your eardrums and make them vibrate. Special bones and nerves in your ears send signals to your brain, and you hear sounds!

FREQUENCY

Every sound wave has a *frequency*. A wave with a high frequency is more, well, frequent: More pulses pass by every second. Low-frequency waves have fewer pulses passing by. Just like length can be measured in units like inches or meters, frequency is measured in a unit called a *hertz*. One hertz is the same as one pulse in a second. 100 hertz means 100 pulses in a second. And so on.

# OF PULSES PER SECOND	AMOUNT IN HERTZ
	1 Hz
1	10 Hz
10	100 Hz
100	1000 Hz
1000	

Ahhh0OOOoOOOOOoooOoo!

PITCH

Pitch is the "highness" or "lowness" of a sound. It's the way we *perceive*, or sense, frequency. Sounds with higher-frequency waves have higher pitch. Sounds with lower-frequency waves have lower pitch. The lowest frequency people can hear is about 20 hertz. The highest is about 20,000 hertz. The lowest note on a piano has a frequency of 27.5 hertz, and the highest note has a frequency of 4,186 hertz.

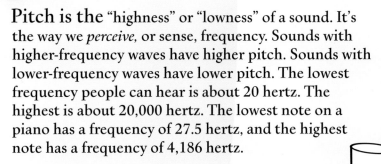

WATER MUSIC

If you clink glasses with different amounts of liquid in them, you'll hear sounds with different pitches. Glasses with more liquid in them will make higher-pitched sounds. Glasses with less liquid in them will make lower sounds. Try it yourself!

LIARS BEWARE! Voice stress analysis is a tool used by some law enforcement agencies to catch people lying. It works like a lie detector machine, but it measures changes in the pitches of people's voices. Some researchers believe that lying causes changes in pitch.

We dogs can hear higher sounds (up to 60,000 Hz)!

VOICES and VIB

Looking down through someone's larynx, you can see the vocal folds.

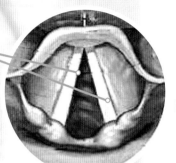

LARYNX

GOOD VIBRATIONS

Sound comes from vibration. Things that make sounds have different vibrating parts. A guitar makes sounds with vibrating strings. A drum makes sounds with a vibrating membrane, or skin.

When you talk or sing, where does the vibration come from? Try a little experiment to find out. *Very gently* put your fingers on the front of your throat. Now talk, sing, or hum. Do you feel the vibration? It comes from your *larynx* (LAIR-inks), also called your voice box. All of the air you breathe passes through your larynx on the way into your lungs and back out again.

You can feel your larynx vibrate when you sing.

your built-in VOICE CHANGER

Your larynx is like a box made of muscles, tendons, and cartilage. Stretched across the inside, where the air passes through, are two membranes called *vocal folds*. They're also called vocal cords, which might make you think they're like strings, but they're really more like a pair of small lips. When you talk or sing, you're using the air you breathe out to make your vocal folds vibrate. The muscles in your larynx can pull the vocal folds apart so the air passes through them easily, or push them together so the air makes them vibrate. Most of the time you're talking, your vocal folds are vibrating.

RATION

ah   ee   oh   oo

CHANGING THE SOUND

You use your lips, tongue, and parts of your throat to change the shape of your vocal tract, that resonating air tube in your head. Try saying, "Ah, ee, oh, oo." Notice the way your lips and tongue move to different places when you make the different sounds.

CHANGING THE PITCH

When I bark, I'm just testing out my larynx.

You use the muscles in your larynx to raise or lower the pitch of your voice.

When the muscles in your larynx stretch the vocal folds so they're tighter, the folds vibrate faster, and the pitch is higher. When the muscles relax the folds so they're looser, the vibration is slower, and the pitch is lower. It's like plucking a tighter rubber band (you get a high-pitched *twing*) or a looser rubber band (you get a lower-pitched *twong*).

On average, kids' voices are higher than grownups', and women's voices are higher than men's. That's because, on average, kids' vocal folds are smaller than grownups', and women's vocal folds are smaller than men's. Smaller vocal folds vibrate faster and have a higher pitch than bigger ones.

That shrimp bubble has so much heat and pressure when it pops that it makes a flash of light!

animal SOUNDS

Sound is used for more than just carrying words through the air to someone's waiting ear. Animals use it in some surprising ways.

CRANK IT UP!

Some animals use loud sounds to stun their prey. A snapping shrimp does it by snapping its claws shut so fast that a bubble forms and then bursts. This "pop!" stuns the shrimp's supper. Researchers aren't sure, but many of them believe that dolphins and sperm whales are also capable of blasting sounds so intense they can stun or even kill their prey.

A snapping shrimp bursts bubbles to stun its prey.

HOW LOW CAN YOU GO?

Elephants communicate with each other with *subsonic* sounds. That means the sounds they make have such low frequencies that we can't even hear them! These low rumbles can travel great distances. Elephant experts think elephants use these rumbles to keep track of each other when they're far apart and out of sight.

▮LAY IT BY EA▮!

Sound can also be used to navigate in strange surroundings. When animals use sound in this way, it's called *sonar*—an abbreviated form of "sound navigation and ranging." Some bats, dolphins, and whales use sonar to find their way around in environments where eyesight just doesn't cut it. At night, bats can't count on their eyes for getting around. It's the same for some animals who live in deep water where sunlight doesn't reach.

Bats can live in groups of thousands, or even millions! Some bats need sonar so they can fly around at night to locate food without crashing into things.

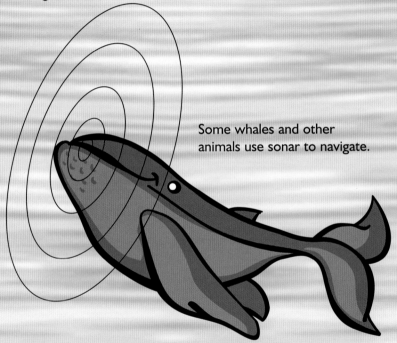

Some whales and other animals use sonar to navigate.

Here's how it works: The animal makes a sound, and the waves travel out. When they hit an obstacle, they bounce back. When the animal hears the echo, it can figure out how far away the obstacle is. This is also called *echolocation* (EH-ko-lo-KAY-shun) because it uses echoes to pinpoint where things are.

Submarine crews use sonar to locate their targets.

how it WORKS

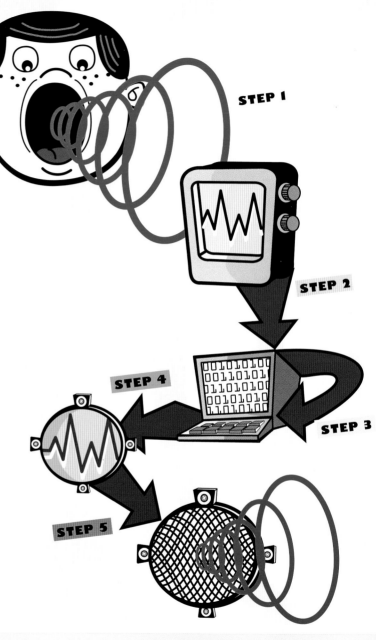

STEP 1

STEP 2

STEP 4

STEP 3

STEP 5

Your electronic Voice Changer works in five steps:

STEP 1

It turns the sound waves of your voice into an electronic signal.

STEP 2

It turns the electronic signals into computer code.

STEP 3

It changes the computer code.

STEP 4

It turns the computer code back into an electronic signal.

STEP 5

It turns the electronic signal back into sound waves.

STEP 1:

SOUND INTO SIGNAL

The part of your Voice Changer that turns the sound waves into an electronic signal is a microphone. The microphone has a membrane, or skin, that acts a lot like your eardrum. When sound waves hit the membrane, the membrane vibrates.

The microphone inside your Voice Changer is a type called a condenser microphone. In condenser microphones, the vibrating membrane is part of a *capacitor*. Capacitors store and release electricity. When the microphone membrane vibrates, it causes changes in the electrical current coming from the capacitor.

The insides of a microphone

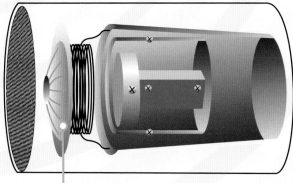

MEMBRANE

VOICE BOX

The first machine that could make sounds that resembled human speech was developed in 1791 by an inventor named Wolfgang von Kempelen. His machine was fitted with bellows to supply the "breath" and reeds that vibrated like vocal folds.

How to Speak Binary

Writing numbers in binary code—also called base 2—is easy:

STEP 2:

Start here →

is there 1 left over?

how many times does 2 go into what's left?

how many times does 4 go into what's le

how many times does 8 go into what's left?

how many times does 16 go into what's left?

how many times does 32 go into what's left?

how many times does 64 go into what's left?

how many times does 128 go into the number?

SIGNALS INTO
COMPUTER CODE

The sound waves of your voice are waves of air pressure. The microphone turns those air-pressure waves into *voltage waves*, which are a little like waves of "electricity pressure." In this step, the signal gets digitized, or turned into a computer code, by a set of circuits called an analog-to-digital (A-D) converter. The A-D converter translates the electronic signal into a series of ones and zeroes. This is called binary code.

WHY BINARY?

The information in binary code can be read and then changed by computers. Your Voice Changer uses programs in a computer chip to change the information in the binary code before it gets turned back into sound.

Try it with 101.

128 goes into 101 no times (0).
64 goes into 101 one time (1) with 37 left over.
32 goes into 37 one time (1) with 5 left over.
16 goes into 5 no times (0).
8 goes into 5 no times (0).
4 goes into 5 one time (1) with 1 left over.
2 goes into 1 no times (0).
There is 1 left over. (1)

So 101 in binary is 01100101.
Here's another way to look at it:
0 x 128 and 1 x 64 and 1 x 32 and 0 x 16
and 0 x 8 and 1 x 4 and 0 x 2 and 1 = 101!

Binary code is computer code. It's what computers "understand."

12

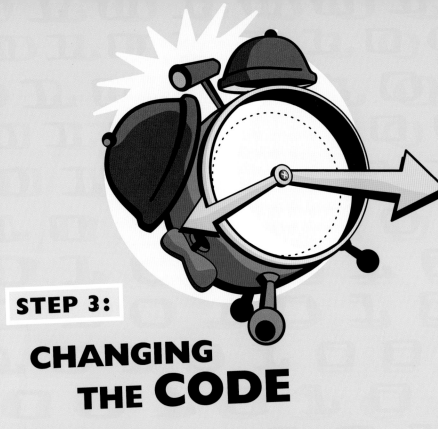

ANALOG and DIGITAL

Analog and digital describe two different kinds of information.

An analog is like a model. The electronic signal is an electronic wave. It's like a copy or a model of a sound wave. If you made a graph of the voltage changes in the electronic wave and a graph of the air pressure changes in the sound wave, the two graphs would be the same.

Digital information is information in the form of numbers. The numbers can describe the measurements of waves, but they're not an exact model of the wave itself.

The difference between analog and digital information is a little bit like the difference between a picture or model of your face and a description of your face in words and measurements.

STEP 3:

CHANGING THE CODE

Once the sound of your voice is converted into digital information, the computer chip and circuits in the Voice Changer can change that information to make the sound effects. It works by doing math on the binary sound code, much like doing a set of calculations on a calculator. The calculations change the information for one set of sound waves into information that creates a different set of sound waves. The Voice Changer does a different set of calculations depending on which of the four voice effects you choose.

how it WORKS

COMPUTER CODE INTO SIGNALS

To play the new, changed sound of your voice, your Voice Changer now has to do everything in reverse. The first step is to convert the computer code for the new sound into an electronic signal. That happens in the digital-to-analog converter, or D-A converter.

DO YOU READ ME?

Talking machines aren't found only in sci-fi movies. They have real, practical uses right here and now. For instance, there are machines that can read books aloud to blind people. The machine scans a page and "figures out" what the letters and words are. Then it reads them out the same way a human would.

Stay sharp!
Try converting these binary numbers into regular base 10 numbers:

01100111

10001100

01000010

The answers are down there at the bottom.

(See page 12 for help.)

01000010 = 66
(0x128 and 1x64 and 0x32 and 0x16 and 0x8 and 0x4 and 1x2 and 0x1 = 66)

10001100 = 140
(1x128 and 0x64 and 0x32 and 0x16 and 1x8 and 1x4 and 0x2 and 0x1 = 140)

01100111 = 103
(0x128 and 1x64 and 1x32 and 0x16 and 0x8 and 1x4 and 1x2 and 1x1 = 103)

STEP 5: SIGNALS INTO SOUND

Finally, the electronic signal gets changed back into sound waves. The electronic signal isn't very strong, so before it's changed back, it gets amplified, or made stronger. Then the speaker turns the amplified signal into sound waves.

The amplified electronic signal goes through the speaker, making a magnet vibrate. The magnet is attached to a shallow cone made of cardboard. When the magnet vibrates, the paper cone vibrates with it. The cone pushes against the molecules of air in front of it, creating sound waves. The sound waves travel to your ears, and you hear your changed voice!

It takes a **lot** of words to describe what happens inside your Voice Changer, but all of the five steps happen almost **instantly**. That's because it's all done with electricity, and electricity moves at the speed of light (about 186,000 miles a **second**)!

MAGNET

CONE

EXPERIMENTS

BANG and BOUNCE

YOU'LL NEED:
- A bowl
- Plastic wrap
- A big rubber band
- Uncooked rice
- A small saucepan and a spoon

Lay the plastic wrap over the top of the bowl, covering it. Press the edges down against the outside of the bowl. Seal it with the big rubber band. Sprinkle a little uncooked rice onto the plastic wrap.

Bang the saucepan with the spoon very close to the bowl. The sound waves from the banging make the rice bounce!

KAZOO

YOU'LL NEED:
- A cardboard tube (like from a roll of toilet paper)
- Wax paper
- Scissors
- A rubber band

Carefully cut out a square of wax paper a little bigger than the opening in the tube. Press the wax paper square against the opening in the tube and fold the edges over the sides of the tube. With the rubber band, secure the wax paper over the end of the tube.

Talk into the open end of the tube. What do you hear? The wax paper vibrates when the sound waves of your voice reach it. Some sounds are amplified, or made louder. You just made a simple voice changer!

THE EAR of a GIANT

YOU'LL NEED:
- The biggest piece of construction paper you can find
- Tape

Roll the construction paper into a cone. Adjust your cone until one end is about as big across as a dime, and the other end flares out as wide as you can manage. Tape the cone so it doesn't unroll itself.

Hold the small end of the cone to your ear—not in your ear—and listen to sounds. You're able to hear quieter sounds than usual because the cone gathers up more sound waves and sends them right into your ear.

BARK IN THE DARK

This one works best with a bunch of friends. Sit in a circle in the dark — or have everyone promise to keep their eyes shut. Pass the Voice Changer around the circle. Whenever anyone wants to, instead of passing the Voice Changer, they say something into it. Can you guess who's talking? (Can you tell what they're saying?)

GOOD NEWS

Who says the newspaper is boring? It sure isn't when you read articles out loud into the Voice Changer. Even the weather report from West Cucumber is enjoyable when read with the Voice Changer set to position 1 (squeaky voice). Find your own ways to liven up the news.

VOICE CHANGER THEATRE

Put on a show for parents, friends, or even paying customers. What makes your performance special is that all the actors speak their lines through the Voice Changer. The bad guy in the show speaks through the Voice Changer using position 3 (the scary voice). The hero uses position 4 (the booming voice). The robot — make sure you write a part for a robot character — uses position 2 (the robotic voice). Don't forget to sign autographs.

ASSEMBLY INSTRUCTIONS

BEFORE YOU BEGIN ASSEMBLING YOUR VOICE CHANGER

You will need...

- One 9-volt battery
- Masking tape or clear tape
- Adult help (if you're under 10)

Now remove the parts from the plastic tray.

Here we go!

① CONNECT the RESISTOR

The resistor (re-ZIS-ter) is the tube-shaped piece with two purple legs.

The resistor reduces the flow of electricity to the other electronic parts. The components in the Voice Changer only need a little bit of electricity. Without a resistor, some of the components would receive too much electricity, and they'd be ruined. Most resistors have a material called carbon inside them. Electricity can't flow easily through carbon.

Think of it like this:

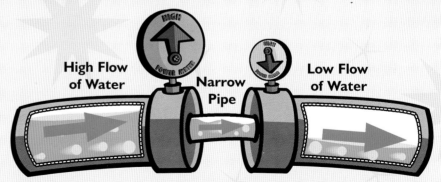

High Flow of Water — Narrow Pipe — Low Flow of Water

Resisitors limit the amount of electricity that flows through parts of a circuit, like a narrow pipe limits water flow.

Here's what you do:

★ Wrap a piece of tape around the top of the resistor. The tape should cover the tube and all of the bare metal.

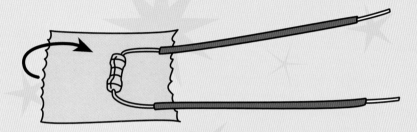

★ Connect one of the resistor's purple wires to one of the circuit board's purple wires. (It doesn't matter which one.) To do this, twist the copper wires together. (See the box to the right, "How to Connect Two Wires.")

The circuit board is the flat, green rectangle screwed into the top case. It has colored wires attached to it.

★ Connect the other two purple wires.

★ Cover each of the connections (the bare wires) with tape.

HOW TO CONNECT TWO WIRES

• Gently straighten and separate the wires on the green circuit board. (Do not wiggle the wires too much or they will break.)

• To connect the wires, simply twist their metal ends together. Make sure you twist both wires around each other.

• To test your connections, gently pull on the wires. They should not come apart.

• Take a piece of tape and wrap it around the bare metal. The tape is the "insulator." It will keep the bare metal from touching other bare metal.

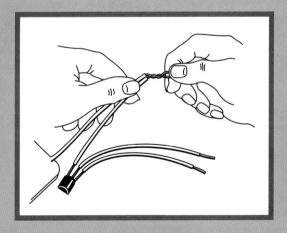

2 CONNECT the TRANSISTOR

The transistor (tran-ZIS-ter) is the little black cylinder with a blue, an orange, and a green wire.

The transistor controls how much electricity passes through your Voice Changer. Electricity flows in one wire (the collector), and out another (the emitter). The middle wire (the base) controls how much electricity flows through.

Think of it like this:

Transistors control how much electricity flows through a circuit.

Here's what you do:

★ Spread the transistor's three wires. The silver metal at the top of the wires should not touch. Wrap a piece of tape around the top. The tape should cover the cylinder and all of the bare metal.

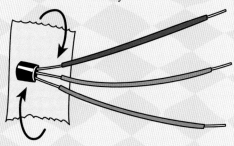

★ Connect the transistor's blue wire to the circuit board's blue wire.

★ Connect the orange wires.

★ Connect the green wires. Be sure you've connected blue to blue, orange to orange, and green to green. If you connect the wrong wires, your Voice Changer won't work.

★ Cover each of the connections (the bare wires) with tape.

We're halfway done!

3 CONNECT the CAPACITOR

The capacitor (ca-PA-se-ter) is a black cylinder with brown and white wires.

Your Voice Changer produces an electric signal that's always changing. The capacitor helps to make the current steady as it flows.

Think of it like this:

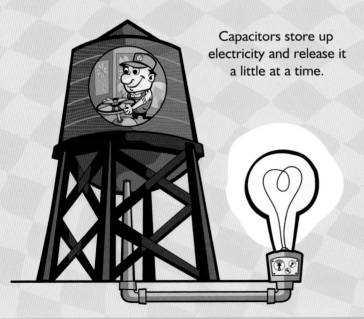

Capacitors store up electricity and release it a little at a time.

Here's what you do:

★ Spread the capacitor's two wires. The silver metal at the top of the wires should not touch. Wrap a piece of tape around the top. The tape should cover the cylinder and all of the bare metal.

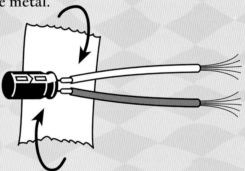

★ Connect the capacitor's brown wire to the circuit board's brown wire.

★ Connect the white wires. Be sure you've connected brown to brown and white to white.

★ Cover each of the connections (the bare wires) with tape.

④ CONNECT the SPEAKER

The speaker is the disk-shaped piece with two yellow wires.

The speaker changes electrical signals into sounds. Inside the speaker is a special magnet called an electromagnet. When electricity flows through the wire to the electromagnet, it makes the electromagnet vibrate. When the electromagnet vibrates, it makes the speaker's cardboard cone move. That movement makes sound.

Here's what you do:

★ Connect one of the speaker's yellow wires to one of the circuit board's yellow wires. (It doesn't matter which one.)

★ Connect the other two yellow wires.

★ Cover each of the connections (the bare wires) with tape.

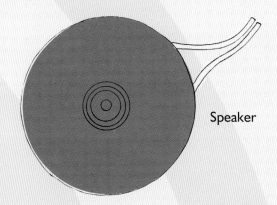

Speaker

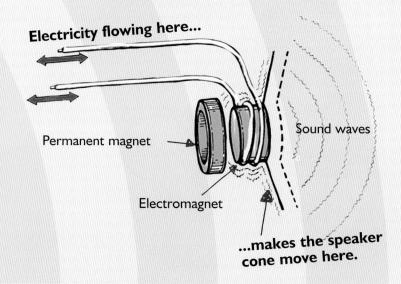

Electricity flowing here...

Permanent magnet

Sound waves

Electromagnet

...makes the speaker cone move here.

TESTING your VOICE CHANGER

Here's what you do:

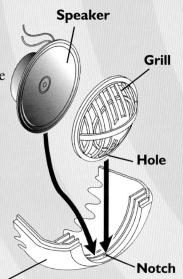

Speaker

Grill

Hole

Notch

Top case

★ Put the yellow grill into the outside groove in the top case. (The top case is the one with the yellow buttons.) The little hole in the bottom of the grill will fit into a notch in the case.

★ Put the speaker into the inside groove in the top case. Make sure the yellow wires stick up. The small end of the speaker should point toward the circuit board.

★ Attach the battery cap to your 9-volt battery.

★ Hold your Voice Changer in front of your mouth like a trumpet and press the yellow button on the top of the case. Speak into the microphone. If your Voice Changer doesn't work, make sure: 1) you've connected the wires together correctly, 2) all the bare metal is covered with tape, and 3) your battery is new.
Take care of the problem before you go on.

Almost done!
Can you feel it?

⑥ PUT it TOGETHER

You've twisted and taped wires, you've learned about electronic components, you've tested your connections and batteries. Now it's time to put the finishing touches on your Voice Changer.

★ Slide the battery into the rectangular box in the bottom case. The battery cap should point toward the speaker. If necessary, put a piece of tape over the battery to keep it in place.

★ Gently tuck the wires inside the case.

★ Line up the speaker and the grill grooves in the top and bottom cases.

★ Carefully snap the cases together.

★ Press and hold the yellow button and speak into the microphone.

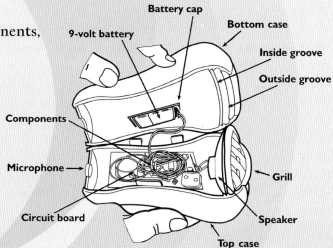

Battery cap
9-volt battery
Bottom case
Inside groove
Outside groove
Components
Microphone →
Grill
Circuit board
Speaker
Top case

Putting the cases together

Bottom case

Top case

Yes! Now get out there and change your voice!

CHANGING your VOICE

There is a yellow sliding switch on the top of your Voice Changer. Slide the switch to one of four positions:

Position 1: Squeaky Voice
Position 2: Robotic Voice
Position 3: Scary Voice
Position 4: Booming Voice

HOLD it LIKE THIS!